Great Journeys Across Earth

BURTON AND SPEKE'S SOURCE OF THE NILE QUEST

Daniel Gilpin

Heinemann Library
Chicago, Illinois

Produced for Heinemann Library by
Monkey Puzzle Media Ltd.

Designed by Patrick Nugent and Victoria Bevan.

Originated by Modern Age.
Printed and bound in China

12 11 10 09 08
10 9 8 7 6 5 4 3 2 1

**Library of Congress Cataloging-in-Publication
Data**
Gilpin, Daniel.
   Burton and Speke's source of the Nile quest /
Daniel Gilpin. -- 1st ed.
      p. cm. -- (Great journeys across earth)
   Includes bibliographical references and index.
   ISBN-13: 978-1-4034-9752-9 (hb) --
   ISBN-13: 978-1-4034-9760-4 (pb)
1. Burton, Richard Francis, Sir, 1821-1890--
Travel--Nile River--Juvenile literature. 2. Speke,
John Hanning, 1827-1864--Travel--Nile River--
Juvenile literature. 3. Nile River--Discovery and
exploration--Juvenile literature. I. Title.
DT117.G55 2007
916.204'09034--dc22

                    2007005830

Acknowledgments
The author and publisher are grateful to the
following for permission to reproduce copyright
material: Alamy pp. **22–23** (Sue Cunningham
Photographic), **34–35** (Blickwinkel), **39** (Nick
Greaves); Corbis pp. **14–15** (Ed Kashi), **18** (Craig
Lovell); Getty Images pp. **5** (The Image Bank), **6**
(Hulton Archive), **18** (Tom Stoddart Archive), **21,
33, 37** (Taxi), **40**; Mary Evans Picture Library pp.
8, 30, 36; MPM Images pp. **13** (Digital Vision),
27 (Digital Vision); Royal Geographical Society
pp. **7, 31**; Science Photo Library pp. **20** (Worldsat
International/J. Knighton), **23 top** (Peter Schoones);
Still Pictures pp. **9** (Mathieu Laboureur), **10** (Joerg
Boethling), **12** (Sean Sprague), **17** (Martin Harvey),
24 (BIOS/Gunther Michel); Topfoto pp. **1** (The Print
Collector/HIP) **11, 25, 26** (The Print Collector/HIP),
28, 34 top, 38.

Maps by Martin Darlison at Encompass Graphics.

Cover photograph of waterfalls on the Nile River
reproduced with permission of Corbis
(Torleif Svensson).

Title page picture: John Hanning Speke painted
this picture of one of the rivers that flow into
Lake Victoria, East Africa.

Expert read by Rob Bowden, geography and
education consultant.

Contents

Some words are shown in bold, **like this**. You can find out what they mean by looking in the glossary.

A Brush with Death

On April 19, 1855, in the East African country of Somalia, two British explorers woke to the sound of bloodcurdling screams. All around them were men armed with spears. The explorers' camp was under attack!

Narrow escape

The explorers scrambled from their tents in the darkness. They would have to fight their way out or die. Their team of **porters** and soldiers fought with them, but there were too many attackers. Many men were injured or killed.

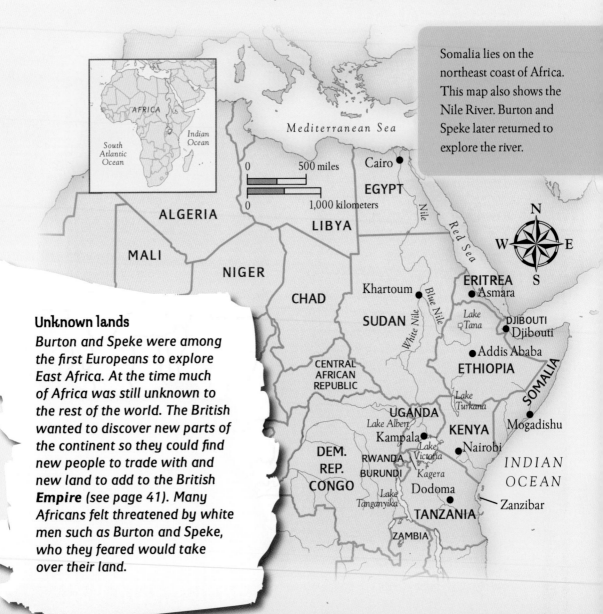

Somalia lies on the northeast coast of Africa. This map also shows the Nile River. Burton and Speke later returned to explore the river.

Unknown lands

Burton and Speke were among the first Europeans to explore East Africa. At the time much of Africa was still unknown to the rest of the world. The British wanted to discover new parts of the continent so they could find new people to trade with and new land to add to the British Empire (see page 41). Many Africans felt threatened by white men such as Burton and Speke, who they feared would take over their land.

One of the explorers, Richard Burton, charged at the attackers with his **saber**. The other, John Speke, used a pistol. Speke shot down several men, but then ran out of bullets and was captured. Burton was hit in the head by a spear, with the blade going in one cheek and out the other. Amazingly, both men survived. Speke was badly wounded, but managed to escape. Burton broke free with the spear still piercing his face.

Ready to return

This frightening experience in Somalia did not stop Burton and Speke from visiting Africa again. Before long, they were ready for another adventure—a journey to discover the **source** (starting point) of the Nile River.

What is the Nile?

The Nile is the longest river in the world. It flows through much of northeast Africa and empties into the Mediterranean Sea. From its farthest source to its **mouth** *(end), the Nile measures some 4,160 miles (6,695 kilometers), although this was not known in Burton and Speke's time. On its journey the Nile travels through seven different countries: Burundi, Tanzania, Rwanda, Uganda, Sudan, Ethiopia, and Egypt.*

The Nile was, and still is, an important transportation route. *Feluccas* (sailing boats) like these have carried goods along the river for centuries. There were no roads or railroads in Africa when Burton and Speke visited.

Preparing to Go

Richard Burton was first asked to explore the Nile in 1856. The **Royal Geographical Society**, an organization based in London, England, planned and paid for the **expedition**. They asked Burton to choose a partner to travel with him. Burton picked his old friend John Speke.

A perfect team

In addition to being explorers, Burton and Speke were military men. They were both captains in charge of many soldiers. Their experience and training made them natural leaders and ideal to command a large expedition to Africa.

The Royal Geographical Society

The Royal Geographical Society (RGS) was set up in London in 1830 to encourage interest and progress in geography. Over the years, it has supported and paid for the expeditions of many scientists and explorers. These include Charles Darwin, Dr. David Livingstone, and Captain Robert Scott, who all became famous for different discoveries. The RGS still exists today.

Richard Burton was born in the English seaside town of Torquay, Devon, in 1821. By the time this picture was taken in 1864, he was 43 years old.

Earlier claims
Burton and Speke were not the first men to look for the source of the Nile. In 1768 a Scottish explorer named James Bruce set off through Egypt and Ethiopia. In 1770 he arrived at Lake Tana, which he claimed was where the Nile began. But Bruce had actually discovered the source of the Blue Nile—another river that joins the Nile at Khartoum in Sudan (see page 41).

Like Burton, John Speke came from Devon, in England. He was born in the town of Bideford. This painting shows Speke in Africa.

Planning the trip

An early suggestion was for Burton and Speke to start their expedition in Cairo, Egypt, and travel up the Nile to reach its **source**. But the Royal Geographical Society figured out that this would take too long and cost too much. They decided that instead, the men should sail to the shores of East Africa and march inland. The journey would begin on the island of Zanzibar, just off the East African coast.

Before they set off, Burton and Speke studied maps of the area they were traveling to. Few Europeans had visited this part of Africa before, and those who had were not accurate mapmakers. Most of the maps they had drawn were based on stories told by local people. Part of Burton and Speke's mission would be to take measurements of the land they covered so that better maps could be made.

An African stepping stone

One part of Africa that was well known to Europeans in Burton and Speke's time was the coast. Lying just off the East African coastline, Zanzibar was the perfect place for Burton and Speke to start their expedition. People there had been trading with the British for decades. Some people spoke English, and they could be hired to work as **translators** and guides for the journey.

Burton and Speke arrived in Zanzibar in time for New Year's 1857. A powerful **sultan** ruled the island. He was interested in Burton and Speke's expedition and invited them to visit his palace. The sultan provided a boat to transport the explorers and their team to the mainland.

In Burton and Speke's time, Zanzibar was a very busy place. Traders came here from all over the world to buy African goods as well as slaves.

The slave trade

In the 18th and 19th centuries, many African people were captured and sent abroad as slaves. Many were sent on ships from Zanzibar. Slaves had no rights and were forced to work. Slavery was banned in Great Britain in 1833 and in the United States in 1865. Burton and Speke explored Africa just as the slave trade was ending.

Before they could leave Zanzibar, Burton and Speke had a lot to do. The most important thing was to find men to make the journey with them. They hired **porters** to carry equipment such as tents, scientific instruments, food, and gifts for tribes whose land they crossed. They also paid a group of soldiers from Baluchistan (now in Pakistan) to accompany them for protection.

Ivory trading
Elephants' tusks are made of ivory, a valuable material that can be carved into fine ornaments. In the past, many African elephants were killed for their tusks, and in Burton and Speke's time Zanzibar was a center for the ivory trade. Today, elephants are protected from hunters, and it is against the law in most countries to sell ivory products.

It is illegal to kill elephants for their tusks, but some people still do it. The tusks these rangers have were taken from hunters after they were arrested.

The Adventure Begins

Burton and Speke sailed away from Zanzibar on June 16, 1857. Their crossing to the African mainland was short. Neither man had ever been to this part of Africa before. They were excited and took notes about everything they saw.

First port

The **expedition** landed at a town called Bagamoyo, on the coast of what is now Tanzania. Burton had learned some of the local language, **Swahili**, in Zanzibar. He found out that Bagamoyo's name came from the Swahili words *bwaga moyo*, which means "throw down your heart." It expressed the heartbreak and terror felt by people there during the slave trade. Bagamoyo was the last place in Africa many people saw.

Bagamoyo has many large old buildings. The town was built in the 18th and 19th centuries using money from the slave trade.

Marching inland

On June 27 the travelers left Bagamoyo and began marching inland. There were nearly 200 men in total, including Africans and Asians as well as the two Englishmen. Local people found them an extraordinary sight. The explorers relied on their trusty guide from Zanzibar, Sidi Mubarak. He knew the land well and helped them to avoid swamps and other hazards.

June is the coolest month in this part of Africa. Even so, it felt hot and sticky to the Englishmen. Also, they were setting off just after the long rainy season. Thick vegetation that had grown up in the wet months slowed the walkers down.

Rainy seasons

Eastern Africa has rainy seasons and dry seasons. During the rainy seasons it is very wet. Land becomes swampy and flooded, and many diseases spread (see pages 14–15). This makes travel very difficult and dangerous.

Eastern Africa has two rainy seasons every year. One lasts from March to May and the other from October to December.

Sidi Mubarak

*Sidi Mubarak (above) was an African from the Yao tribe who worked as a guide and **translator** for the expedition. When he was hired, in Zanzibar, he was just 18 years old. Mubarak spoke the Indian language Hindustani (which Burton understood) as well as Swahili. When he was older, he wrote about his adventures with the two explorers, and about the travels he made with Speke and James Grant a few years later (see page 34).*

Worrying whispers

Traveling through the coastal **plains**, the explorers had to hack their way through giant thickets of grass using huge knives called **machetes**. Before long, everyone was exhausted. One evening, Burton overheard some of the soldiers plotting against him and Speke. They were saying they should steal the valuable gifts the **porters** were carrying and run away. Burton did not want to confront the soldiers, in case they tried to kill him. So, he decided to wait and see what would happen.

Paying to pass

As the explorers headed southwest from the coast, Speke noticed that some places were planted with crops. Nearby there were villages of round huts with cone-shaped grass roofs. The local people belonged to a tribe called the Wazaramo. Wazaramo men stopped the expedition by standing in the way with bows and poisoned arrows. Their chieftains were the first to demand *hongo* (see box below) from Burton and Speke.

Hongo

As Burton and Speke traveled, they crossed land controlled by different tribes. The chiefs of these tribes demanded payment before they would let travelers pass. This payment was known as hongo. Instead of money, it was paid with gifts such as beads, brass wire, and cloth.

Cone-roofed houses are still found on Tanzania's coastal plains. People live and farm there much as they did in Burton and Speke's time.

Kilimanjaro, Africa's highest mountain, lies in the Great Rift Valley. The area is rich in wildlife, including giraffes.

The Great Rift Valley

The area Burton and Speke covered was part of the Great Rift Valley. This runs up eastern Africa, from Mozambique to northern Ethiopia, and extends as far as Jordan in Arabia. The Rift Valley marks the dividing line between two of Earth's plates. Plates are sections of Earth's crust (surface layer) that float on a mass of very hot rock called the mantle. Rift valleys form when two plates move very slowly apart. As they do so, the bottom of the gap is filled by melted rock from the mantle. Sometimes this bursts out in volcanic eruptions.

Sickness strikes

As the expedition continued, Burton fell ill with a powerful **fever**. He became so weak that he could not walk. Speke watched over his companion until, gradually, he began to recover. Burton was not the only member of the expedition to suffer. Many of the porters and some of the soldiers also fell sick, and a few of them died.

Medicine in Burton and Speke's time was still very basic and many diseases were not yet understood. Later in the journey, Speke almost completely lost his sight to a mystery illness before eventually getting better. Experts now think he might have been suffering from river blindness, a disease common in Africa but unknown to Europeans then. River blindness is passed on by biting blackflies, which live near fast-flowing streams.

Malaria

*Burton suffered from a disease called malaria. Malaria is spread by mosquitoes and is common in **tropical** parts of the world. Some types of malaria can kill but most, including the type Burton had, just make people very ill. If it is not cleared out of the body with drugs, the fever and other symptoms can return from time to time, making the person suffer all over again.*

Many people in Africa drink and wash in river water. If the water is polluted then diseases can spread easily.

Scary smallpox

As the explorers marched on, they found native people suffering from another illness – smallpox. This deadly disease was common in many parts of the world in the 19th century, but no longer exists. In 1979, the **World Health Organization** announced that it had completely wiped out smallpox with a **vaccine** – a treatment that stopped people catching the disease.

Medical kit

One of the few medicines the explorers took with them on their trip was quinine. This was used to treat malaria. They also carried bandages, as well as alcohol and **opium***, which were used as painkillers.*

Into the Mountains

After more than a month, the explorers reached the edge of the coastal **plains** and began to march uphill. Slowly, their surroundings changed from grassland into forest.

Trouble at the camp

As they climbed, Burton and Speke noticed the air was cooler. This made marching easier, and so they began to cover more ground. Before long the men reached the hill town of Morogoro at the base of the Uluguru Mountains. Here, they set up camp.

After marching over the coastal plains, Burton and Speke's expedition had to cross over mountains.

The boiling thermometer

As Burton and Speke traveled, they took measurements of the land for mapmaking. One important measurement was **altitude** *(height above sea level). Burton and Speke figured out how high they were by boiling a pot of water, then measuring its temperature with a thermometer. Water boils at lower temperatures as air pressure drops. Air pressure is the amount of air weighing down on something from above. It is lower at high altitudes than at sea level because the distance up to space (where there is no air) is less.*

Lake Victoria

SERENGETI PLAIN

KENYA

Wembere

Mount Kilimanjaro 19,340 ft (5,895 m)

INDIAN OCEAN

GREAT RIFT VALLEY

MAASAI STEPPE

Pangani

Pemba

TANZANIA

Zanzibar

Dodoma

Bagamoyo

RUBEHO MOUNTAINS

Morogoro

Dar es Salaam

ULUGURU MOUNTAINS

COASTAL LOWLANDS

Rufiji

Mafia

MBARIKA MOUNTAINS

Lake Malawi

0   100 miles

0   200 kilometers

N
W   E
S

The scenery was impressive, with slopes of thick forest looming above. But Burton and Speke were unable to relax. Over the past week, some of the **porters** had disappeared and stolen valuable baggage. Now it looked like the soldiers were plotting again. Within hours of arriving at Morogoro, Burton's worst fears came true. The soldiers **mutinied**. They all drew pistols, but no one was hurt. The soldiers took what they wanted and left the camp.

From Morogoro, Burton and Speke's **expedition** continued through the hills. More porters abandoned them on the way, disappearing in the dark of night. But others, including Sidi Mubarak, remained loyal. Ahead of them, getting closer day by day, were the dark ridges of the Rubeho Mountains.

Bushbabies are common in the East African mountain forests. These little creatures were named for the cries that they make in the night.

Tanzania's mountain forest
The Rubeho Mountains are covered in thick forest. Scientists are still exploring the forests today. They note the different animals and plants they find there, such as the red-bellied coast squirrel and the rare Zanj elephant shrew. In 2005 an entirely new species (type) of bird was found there—the Rubeho forest partridge.

Savannah country

Traveling through the Rubeho Mountains was hard work. The jungle was dense, and it took them almost a month to get through. But finally the men began to climb downhill. As they left the forest, they discovered a huge, grassy plain. This type of land is known as **savannah**. The sunlight was strong, and the men took a few days to get used to marching without the shade of any trees.

Burton and Speke headed southwest a little before crossing the savannah. They did this to avoid trouble with the Maasai (see box below). As they marched, they saw herds of grass-eating animals, including zebras, wildebeests, and Cape buffalo. Sometimes they saw elephants or dangerous meat-eaters, such as lions and hyenas. Guards had to keep watch over the camp by night.

The Maasai people live by herding goats and cattle. Many of the men carry large spears to protect their animals from lions and other hunters.

The Maasai tribe

The Maasai people live on the plains of Kenya and Tanzania. Today, they are peaceful, but in Burton and Speke's time they were a powerful and dangerous tribe. They controlled most of the grassy savannah and attacked and killed strangers who wandered onto their land. The Maasai fought with spears. They also used spears to kill lions and other animals that hunted their livestock.

The savannah was flat, and there was no rain because it was now the dry season. But it was still cooler here than on the coast. This is because the savannah lay on a raised area of land called a **plateau**—around 3,000 feet (900 meters) above sea level. At high altitudes like this, temperatures drop, as in the mountains.

A place to rest

After several weeks of marching through the savannah, Burton and Speke saw a welcome sight in the distance—the city of Tabora. They had known it would be here and were looking forward to stopping for some good food and a well-earned rest.

Prowling lions

*Lions were a constant danger to Burton and Speke's expedition. These big cats live in groups called **prides**, led by one or two adult males. Most lion prides contain several females, known as lionesses. Lionesses do nearly all of the hunting, working together to catch other animals to eat.*

Tanzania is famous for its savannah, which is home to huge numbers of animals. Here, a lioness watches a herd of wildebeest.

Toward the Inland Sea

Burton and Speke arrived in Tabora on November 7, 1857. After months of hard walking and camping, a real bed to rest in seemed like luxury. For some of the **porters**, the break was especially exciting because Tabora was their home.

New information

Tabora was the largest **settlement** in the **savannah**. It was home to a mix of people, including many Arabs. Burton spoke Arabic well—he had learned it on previous travels. He soon heard some interesting news. According to the Arabs, the "inland sea" the men were searching for was not one stretch of water but three: the Sea of Niassa (which lay to the south), the Sea of Ujiji (to the west), and the Sea of Ukerewe (to the north). From its location, Burton thought that the Sea of Ujiji (now Lake Tanganyika) was probably the **source** of the Nile.

This satellite picture clearly shows the "inland seas" Burton and Speke sought. The three "seas" are now known as Lake Victoria, Lake Tanganyika, and Lake Malawi.

Lake Tanganyika

Lake Tanganyika is the world's sixth largest lake and the second biggest lake in Africa (after Lake Victoria). It is around 420 miles (678 kilometers) long and covers an area about the size of Maryland. It is also the world's second deepest lake. Lake Tanganyika is shared among four countries: Burundi, Tanzania, Zambia, and the Democratic Republic of the Congo.

In December the team set off to the west. During the journey, Speke's eyesight, which had been bad for some weeks, suddenly started to get worse. By the time they reached the Sea of Ujiji, in February 1858, he could hardly see at all. Burton, on the other hand, found an amazing view. The sheet of water was enormous, stretching as far as the eye could see.

Burton in Mecca
*Before exploring Africa, Burton made many other famous journeys. He was one of the first Europeans to enter the holy Muslim city of Mecca, in what is now Saudi Arabia. Muslims are people who follow the religion of Islam. Mecca contains the Sacred **Mosque**, Islam's holiest site. Today, Islam is one of the largest religions on Earth, with more than a billion followers.*

When he was in Arabia, Richard Burton wore the same clothes as local people. This helped him blend in when he visited Mecca.

Exploring Lake Tanganyika's banks

If Lake Tanganyika was the source of the Nile, there would have to be a large river pouring out of it. The lake was so big that it could take months to search its banks on foot. The only boats the explorers could find were dugout canoes, which were made by hollowing out large logs.

Speke went off to look for a bigger boat, but he found nothing. One night while he was away, he woke up covered in beetles. One beetle crawled into his ear and got stuck. Try as he might, Speke could not get it out, even with a knife. The beetle died, rotted, and caused a bad infection. Now Speke, who was already half blind, became deaf in one ear.

Taking to the water

Speke's disabilities did not stop him from rowing a canoe. He returned to Burton, and together they began to paddle. They knew the Nile flowed northward, so they headed for the north end of the lake. However, local men with their own canoes stopped Burton and Speke on their way. The explorers were forced to turn back, landing at a village on the eastern shore.

Burton and Speke tried to explore Lake Tanganyika in canoes made from hollowed-out logs, similar to the ones shown here.

The iron boat

Burton and Speke set off from Zanzibar with a large iron boat to explore the inland sea they expected to find. The boat was transported in seven parts, which they could easily fit together. But the porters soon found the load too heavy, and they left it behind not far from the African coast.

Villagers told the Englishmen that there was a large river to the north, but the water flowed into the lake, not out of it. Burton and Speke knew this could not be the Nile, because the Nile would be flowing away from the lake, starting its long journey toward the sea. The river the villagers talked about was in fact the Rusizi. There was no other river at this end of the lake. So, Lake Tanganyika could not be the source of the Nile after all.

These colorful fish are known as cichlids. Today, there are more than 250 different species (types) of cichlids living in Lake Tanganyika.

Evolution in action

About 12 million years ago, Lake Tanganyika, which was once a part of the Indian Ocean, was cut off from the sea by movements in Earth's crust. When this happened, the lake contained just a few types of animals, including sponges, crabs, and jellyfish. Later, various cichlid fish arrived, probably from the Congo River, which runs out of the lake. Since then, the descendants of these fish have slowly evolved (changed) to form many new colorful species.

Time to Think Again

Burton was hugely disappointed to find he was wrong about Lake Tanganyika. He was certain that the **source** of the Nile was in this region. But his **expedition** had failed. Supplies were low, and the explorers had to head back to Tabora.

Leaving the lake

As they prepared to leave, Burton said to Speke that the source of the Nile must lie in the mountains west of the lake. The only way to find it, he thought, would be to follow the Nile upstream from Gondokoro in southern Sudan. No one was known to have done this before. It would be up to a future expedition to attempt it.

Chimpanzees live in large groups, known as troops, and are found only in Africa. They can climb trees well, but are also comfortable on the ground.

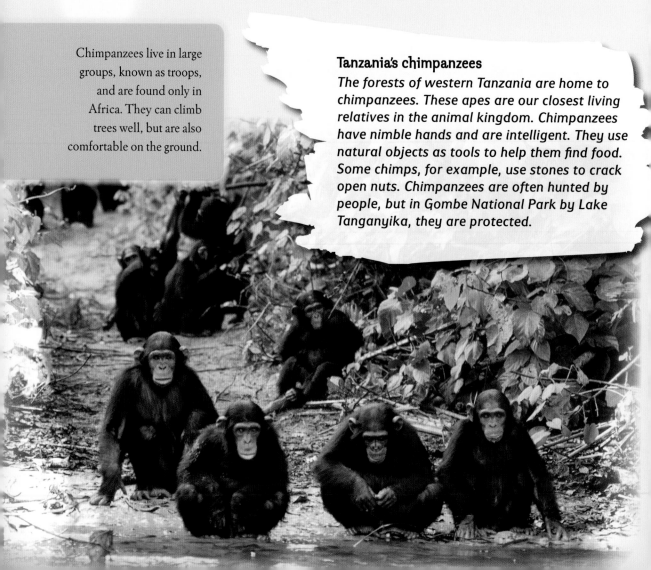

Tanzania's chimpanzees

The forests of western Tanzania are home to chimpanzees. These apes are our closest living relatives in the animal kingdom. Chimpanzees have nimble hands and are intelligent. They use natural objects as tools to help them find food. Some chimps, for example, use stones to crack open nuts. Chimpanzees are often hunted by people, but in Gombe National Park by Lake Tanganyika, they are protected.

Burton and Speke felt gloomy as they made their way back to Tabora. They passed through beautiful hills covered in forest, but the scenery did not cheer them up. After the hills came marshland, then grassy **savannah** again. It was almost a month before the men reached the city.

Back in Tabora, a long rest awaited the travelers. They had been on the move for weeks and were exhausted. On top of that, the wet season was about to begin. This would make the trip back to the coast much more difficult. It would be better to travel homeward in a few months, after the rains had cleared.

In Burton and Speke's time, most buildings in Tabora were made of wood. Today, it is one of the largest towns in central Tanzania.

Rain forest worlds

*Burton and Speke passed through **tropical** rain forest on their journey. Tropical rain forest is home to more types of animals and plants than any other natural **habitat**. It grows in hot, rainy areas around the **Equator**. Sadly, in Africa and elsewhere in the world, tropical rain forest is disappearing fast. People cut down the huge trees that grow in it for timber or burn it to make way for new farmland.*

Rest and restlessness

Over the months in Tabora, Burton and Speke began to feel strong again. Speke's ear infection cleared up and his hearing came back. Gradually, his eyesight returned, too. Burton made many friends among the Arabs in the city and was happy there. But Speke felt restless. He wanted to explore more of this mysterious part of Africa.

A new journey

Speke decided that he should try to find the Sea of Ukerewe (now Lake Victoria). Burton agreed to let him go alone, with a few **porters**. In July 1858 Speke set off across the **plains**, following his **compass** arrow directly north. On August 3 the Sea of Ukerewe came into sight.

Lake Victoria

Speke decided to rename the Sea of Ukerewe after Victoria, the British queen at the time. Lake Victoria is Africa's biggest lake and the third largest lake on Earth. It covers an area of 26,830 square miles (69,489 square kilometers)—slightly more than the size of West Virginia. Compared with other lakes of its size, Lake Victoria is quite shallow. It measures just 275 feet (84 meters) at its deepest point.

In addition to being an explorer, John Speke was an artist. This painting, based on his sketches, shows one of the smaller rivers that flow into Lake Victoria.

Speke was amazed by the size of the "sea" he saw. He tasted the water and found it to be fresh, like river water. He was sure this must be the source of the Nile. He would return to Tabora to collect Burton, then they could come back to look for the start of the river together.

A hippopotamus has an enormous mouth and very large teeth. Although hippos can be dangerous, they live on a diet of grass.

Hippos

The hippopotamus (hippo) is a common sight in many of Africa's lakes and rivers. Speke himself saw them in Lake Victoria. Hippos spend the day in the water and come out at night to eat grass. They are the second biggest animals in Africa, after elephants. An adult male hippo can weigh just over 3 tons (3 tonnes).

Homeward Bound

Back in Tabora, Speke rushed to tell Burton about his exciting discovery. But Burton was unimpressed. He argued that Lake Victoria was too far east to be the **source** of the Nile. Speke could not persuade him to go and explore it.

Farewell to Africa

Before long, Burton and Speke left Tabora and began their journey back to the coast. They had to leave anyway, because their money had almost run out. The two explorers finally reached Bagamoyo at the end of February 1859. There, they quickly found a boat to Zanzibar, arriving on March 4. Speke was eager to get back to Great Britain. He left on the first ship he could find. Meanwhile, Burton sailed up the eastern coast of Africa to Aden in Arabia, and stayed there a little while before also boarding a ship home.

A long way around

Burton and Speke lived long before the age of international flights. People had to travel across seas by boat, and journeys were long and slow. Traveling to Britain from Zanzibar meant sailing all the way around the southern tip of Africa and up through the Atlantic Ocean.

A **steamer** very similar to this one carried Speke back to Britain from Zanzibar. The ships in the background of this picture are traditional sailing ships.

Speke had promised not to say anything about their adventure until both men were back in Britain. But he was angry with Burton for refusing to explore Lake Victoria with him. An old friend of Burton's—a writer and journalist named Laurence Oliphant—was on board the same ship as Speke. The two met up, and soon Speke told Oliphant everything.

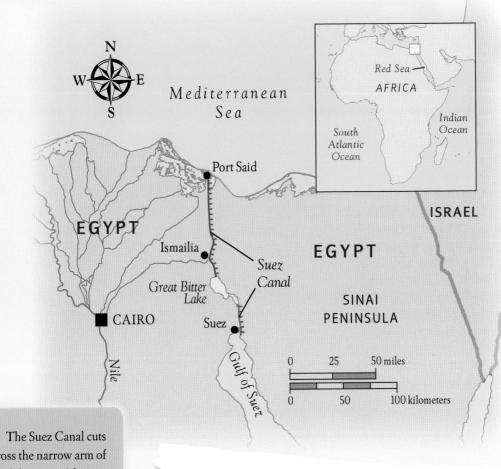

The Suez Canal cuts across the narrow arm of land that joins Africa to Arabia. Before it opened, ships were forced to sail around Africa.

The Suez Canal
The Suez Canal dramatically shortened journeys from Europe to the Indian Ocean. This waterway across northeast Egypt links the Mediterranean to the Red Sea. When Burton and Speke returned to Britain, work on building the Suez Canal was only just beginning. The Canal finally opened in 1869. Today, it is one of the most important and busiest waterways in the world.

Claiming the prize

As soon as Speke arrived in Britain, early in May 1859, he headed to the **Royal Geographical Society** in London. He met up with Sir Roderick Murchison, the society's president, and told him everything. Unlike Burton, Murchison believed Speke's theory about Lake Victoria. The next day the news was officially announced—John Hanning Speke had discovered the source of the Nile.

Man of rocks

Sir Roderick Murchison was 67 when Speke met him at the Royal Geographical Society. In his younger years, he had been a great scientist. Murchison was famous for his discoveries in geology, the study of rocks. In the 1830s, he described rocks from a point in Earth's history that no one had studied before—a time he called the Silurian Period. We now know that the Silurian Period lasted from 438 to 408 million years ago. The rocks he described were formed 200 million years before the first dinosaurs appeared on Earth.

Almost overnight, Speke became one of the most famous people in Britain. Everybody was talking about this previously unknown man and his amazing adventures in Africa. When Burton returned to Britain on May 21, he saw that his chance for glory was gone. He tried to explain that Speke was mistaken, but nobody would listen. People just thought that Burton was jealous of Speke because Speke had found the source of the Nile without him.

Both Burton and Speke were awarded gold medals by the Royal Geographical Society, the society's highest honor. The medals shown here were awarded to other explorers in the 20th century.

Burton heads for the United States

Burton's argument with Speke did not do his reputation any good. In spring 1860, just a few months after he had returned from Africa, he left Britain again. This time Burton set sail for the United States, on a journey to Salt Lake City. He wanted to find out more about the **Mormons,** *people who follow the Mormon religion, which was founded there.*

Return to the Source

While people criticized Burton, Speke became a national hero. His fame even spread around the world. But one thing was still missing from his claim to have discovered the **source** of the Nile. He had not found the beginning of the river, where it poured out of Lake Victoria.

In search of proof

To fully prove Speke's claim, the missing section of river had to be found. So, soon after Burton left for the United States, the **Royal Geographical Society** planned another **expedition** to Lake Victoria. This time they asked Speke to lead the team. He was pleased to accept and chose an old friend, James Augustus Grant, to be his second-in-command.

Speke knew exactly what he would need to take because he had been to Lake Victoria before. He explained his plans to the Royal Geographical Society, and they agreed to pay for everything. They supplied Speke with scientific and mapmaking instruments, which were packed into sturdy crates for the journey. More basic items, such as tents, would be made up later in Zanzibar. Speke would also hire **porters** on the island. Speke and Grant left on a **steamer** from Plymouth, England, on April 27, 1860. They finally arrived in Zanzibar on August 15 that year.

The Cape of Good Hope

On their way to Zanzibar, Speke and Grant stopped and spent 12 days on the Cape of Good Hope, a piece of land jutting out into the sea from South Africa's southwest coast. The Cape was first sighted by the Portuguese explorer Bartolemeu Dias in 1488. He named it Cabo Tormentoso, which literally means "Cape of Storms." Very strong winds often lash the water near the Cape, forming enormous waves. This makes travel by ship there dangerous.

James Augustus Grant

*Grant (see picture) was born in 1827 in the town of Nairn, in northwest Scotland. Like Speke, he was a soldier before becoming an explorer. At the time, Britain had many **trading posts** in India, which sometimes needed protection. Grant worked in the army in India until 1858. Then, he returned to Britain, before joining Speke on his expedition in 1860.*

James Augustus Grant joined Speke as his second-in-command. Unlike Speke, who was a geographer, Grant was interested in biology.

Cross country

Arriving in Zanzibar, Speke and Grant were eager to sail to Bagamoyo and begin their journey inland. But first they had to hire porters, buy supplies, and meet up with other men who had been instructed to go with them. When they finally got to Bagamoyo, they found themselves in charge of more than 150 people. These included 30 soldiers sent by the **sultan** of Zanzibar to escort them some of the way.

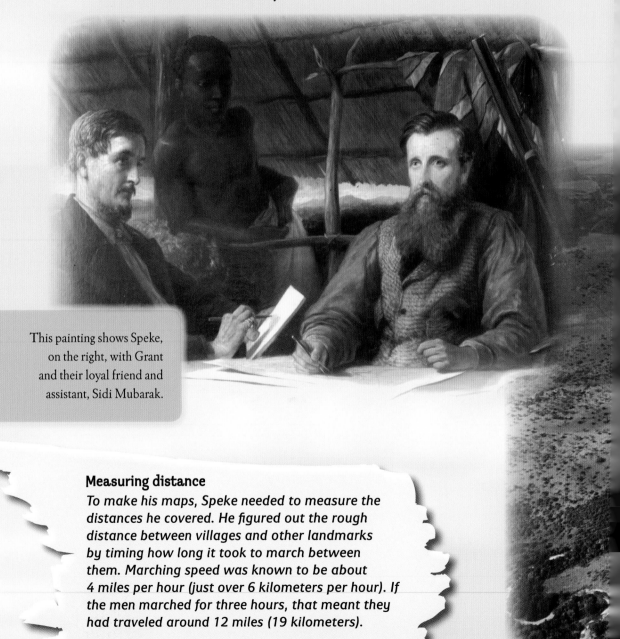

This painting shows Speke, on the right, with Grant and their loyal friend and assistant, Sidi Mubarak.

Measuring distance

To make his maps, Speke needed to measure the distances he covered. He figured out the rough distance between villages and other landmarks by timing how long it took to march between them. Marching speed was known to be about 4 miles per hour (just over 6 kilometers per hour). If the men marched for three hours, that meant they had traveled around 12 miles (19 kilometers).

On September 30 the explorers set off. They traveled first through the lush coastal lowlands, then slowly up into the Rubeho Mountains (see page 17). Their expedition followed a daily routine. The march began before dawn and was over by lunchtime. This way, the men avoided walking during the hottest hours of the day. In the afternoons, Speke made measurements for his maps or went out hunting. Grant spent most of his time studying and drawing the plants and animals that he saw.

For much of the journey, Speke followed the route he had taken with Burton three years earlier. On January 25, 1861, the expedition finally arrived in Tabora. Heavy rains and flooding meant that Speke and Grant would stay in the town for almost two months.

River paths

As Speke and Grant left the flat coastal lowlands and started to climb into the hills, they noticed how the rivers changed. Near the coast, the rivers flowed slowly around great loops, called meanders. In the hills, the rivers were faster and their paths twisted less. Over thousands of years, the fast-flowing rivers had carved out deep, V-shaped valleys. Valleys like this form when rushing water gradually wears away the rock beneath.

The rivers in Tanzania's coastal lowlands twist and turn as they snake slowly toward the sea.

A long struggle

As soon as the rains ended and the land began to dry out, Speke and Grant prepared to leave Tabora. But problems were in store. Many porters left and needed replacing. Grant became sick with a mysterious **tropical** disease. When the expedition finally made progress, they came across lands struck by **famine**. Poor rains the year before meant that the crops had failed, and now there was not enough food. Everywhere, people were starving. Speke and Grant also went hungry. The journey was becoming a huge struggle. Would they ever reach their goal?

Grant's illness eventually forced Speke to travel on alone. It was four months before the two explorers met up again, this time on the southern shores of Lake Victoria. Here, the land was fertile (good for growing crops) and green and there was plenty of food to give the men strength. Speke decided to explore around the lake alone, leaving Grant to investigate the local plants and animals.

Grant became so sick that he was unable to walk. Four strong men carried him when he was at his sickest. A frame covered with thin fabric helped protect him from flies and the burning rays of the Sun.

This species, Grant's gazelle, was named after Grant. This is a male. Female Grant's gazelles have much smaller horns.

Grant's role

Grant was more interested in Africa's plants and animals than in its rivers. He discovered and described many new species. He made detailed notes and drawings of what he saw and collected examples of unusual plants to study back in Britain. Later, Grant wrote a book called **Botany** *of the Speke and Grant Expedition.* It is still used by many scientists today.

Proof at last

On July 28, 1862, Speke finally found what he had been searching for—the place where water poured out of Lake Victoria and the Nile River began. "Here at last I stood on the brink of the Nile," he later wrote. "Most beautiful was the scene, nothing could surpass it!" The place was named Ripon Falls.

Lake Victoria today

Since Speke and Grant's expedition, Lake Victoria has grown. In 1954 a large dam—called the Owen Falls or Nalubaale Dam—was built a little way down the Nile. This blocked the water from flowing from the lake, so the level of the lake's surface rose. Ripon Falls, along with much of the surrounding land, was flooded and hidden underwater. Today, the Nile leaves Lake Victoria through a channel inside the dam.

A meeting in the wilderness

A proud Speke left Ripon Falls and headed downstream to meet Grant. They were both now eager to get home, taking a shortcut across land to the town of Gondokoro (see page 24). Boats would be waiting for them there, ready to take them north to Cairo. In Gondokoro, Speke and Grant were surprised to find two other explorers from England, Samuel Baker and his wife, Florence. They were also in search of the source of the Nile and were disappointed to hear that Speke had beaten them to it.

The Bakers had explored the Nile from Cairo, in Egypt, all the way to the Murchison Falls, in Uganda. They had also explored most of the Blue Nile, which starts in Ethiopia. Their journey, which had begun in March 1861, took them through hot, dry desert and cool mountain highlands. They had also picked their way through the sticky Sudd swamps (see box below right) before meeting Speke and Grant at Gondokoro.

A hero's welcome

When Speke and Grant finally returned to London, they were welcomed as heroes. Speke was already famous, but now the name of James Augustus Grant joined the list of great British explorers. He had found and drawn plants and animals that no Europeans had ever seen before.

Speke and Grant met the Bakers at Gondokoro, in what is now Sudan. In this picture Samuel Baker is sitting on the right and his wife, Florence, is standing between Grant and Speke.

Lake Albert

After meeting Speke, Samuel and Florence Baker went on to discover Lake Albert farther upstream. They named it after Queen Victoria's husband, Prince Albert. It turned out that the Nile flowed about 260 miles (418 kilometers) from Lake Victoria, then poured into Lake Albert. The river then continued its journey to the sea after flowing out the other side.

Although much smaller than Lake Victoria, Lake Albert is still huge. It lies on the border between Uganda and the Democratic Republic of the Congo.

The Sudd swamps

*Just downstream from where Speke and Grant met the Bakers, the Nile hits a great, flat **plain**. Here, the river broadens out to form a massive wetland called the Sudd swamps. During the rainy season, the swamps grow to cover an area almost the size of South Carolina, making them one of the largest wetlands in the world. The Sudd swamps are home to a huge range of unusual animals and birds, including the lechwe antelope, the African lungfish (a fish that breathes air), and the shoebill stork.*

The World Reacts

The journeys of Burton, Speke, Grant, and the Bakers helped to open up Africa to the outside world. They also paved the way for Britain to **conquer** much of Africa's land. In the years to come, most of the countries along the Nile River were taken over by British forces and made part of the British **Empire**.

Speke and Grant returned to Britain as heroes. They told everybody about their adventures at a special welcome party organized by the **Royal Geographical Society**.

Changing hands

By 1898 Britain controlled the whole Nile between Ripon Falls and the Mediterranean Sea. Only Ethiopia and the upper end of the Blue Nile remained outside British rule. The land Burton and Speke traveled through from the coast was conquered first by Germany in the 1880s. But at the end of **World War I** in 1918, Britain took over and it became the British **colony** of Tanganyika (now Tanzania). In the second half of the 20th century, this land and other African countries ruled by Britain and Europe became **independent**. The Africans once again controlled their own lands.

Making history

When Burton, Speke, Grant, and the Bakers made their discoveries, they had no idea that any of this was going to happen. They went to Africa for the adventure, to see sights that few Europeans had seen before. Their names went down in history, but they could not have done what they did without the help of many other people. These included their **porters**, guides, **translators**, and the other explorers and mapmakers who had gone before them.

White or Blue?

From maps today (see page 4) we can see that the Nile forks at Khartoum in Sudan. The river from Lake Victoria to this point is now known as the White Nile. The other branch, which the Bakers explored, is called the Blue Nile. This river flows from Lake Tana in Ethiopia. It is shorter than the White Nile.

The British Empire (colored in pink) became the biggest the world had ever seen—far bigger than the Roman Empire or any other empire before or since.

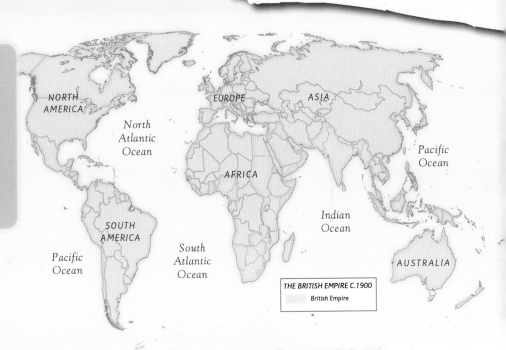

NORTH AMERICA

North Atlantic Ocean

EUROPE

ASIA

AFRICA

Pacific Ocean

Indian Ocean

SOUTH AMERICA

Pacific Ocean

South Atlantic Ocean

AUSTRALIA

THE BRITISH EMPIRE C.1900
British Empire

Measuring the Nile today

Burton, Speke, Grant, and the Bakers greatly increased people's knowledge of the Nile River—but we know even more today. Since Speke found the Nile flowing out of Lake Victoria, people have discovered more about the rivers that flow into the lake. The longest of these is called the Kagera River, which starts in the Nyungwe Forest in Rwanda. Now, when people measure the full length of the Nile, they measure it from the beginning of the Kagera, across Lake Victoria, and all the way to the Mediterranean Sea.

Route to the Source

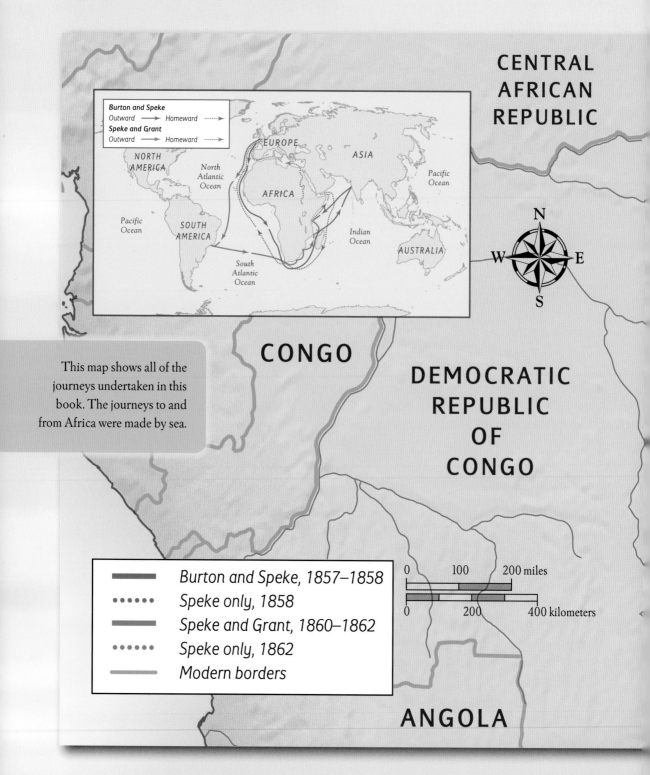

This map shows all of the journeys undertaken in this book. The journeys to and from Africa were made by sea.

Burton and Speke
Outward ⟶ Homeward ┄┄┄┄

Speke and Grant
Outward ⟶ Homeward ┄┄┄┄

NORTH AMERICA

North Atlantic Ocean

EUROPE

ASIA

Pacific Ocean

AFRICA

Pacific Ocean

SOUTH AMERICA

Indian Ocean

South Atlantic Ocean

AUSTRALIA

CENTRAL AFRICAN REPUBLIC

CONGO

DEMOCRATIC REPUBLIC OF CONGO

ANGOLA

━━━━ Burton and Speke, 1857–1858
•••••• Speke only, 1858
━━━━ Speke and Grant, 1860–1862
•••••• Speke only, 1862
━━━━ Modern borders

0   100   200 miles
0   200   400 kilometers

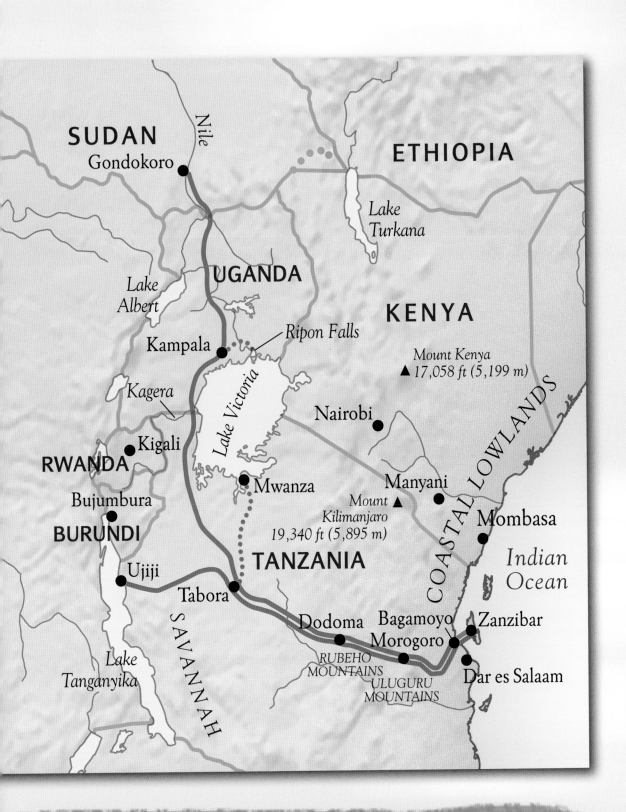

Timeline

November 14, 1770	The Scottish explorer James Bruce arrives at Lake Tana in Ethiopia and claims it is the **source** of the Nile. He is later proved wrong.
1853	Richard Francis Burton becomes the first Englishman to enter the Muslim holy city of Mecca in present-day Saudi Arabia.
April 19, 1855	Burton and John Hanning Speke are attacked while exploring in Somalia, northeast Africa. They are injured, but escape.
1856	Burton is asked by the **Royal Geographical Society** to lead an **expedition** to search for the source of the Nile. He chooses Speke to be his second-in-command.
January 1857	Burton and Speke arrive in Zanzibar and begin preparations for their journey inland.
June 16, 1857	Burton and Speke sail to Bagamoyo on the East African coast. They stay there for just over a week, making final plans.
June 27, 1857	Burton and Speke leave Bagamoyo and start marching inland. With them are nearly 200 other men, including soldiers, **translators**, and **porters** who carry the equipment and supplies.
November 7, 1857	Burton and Speke arrive in Tabora.
December 1857	Burton and Speke leave Tabora to search for the "Sea of Ujiji" (Lake Tanganyika), which Burton thinks is the source of the Nile.
February 1858	Burton and Speke finally discover Lake Tanganyika. They explore the lake to see if a large river flows out of it, but find nothing. They head back to Tabora.
July 1858	Speke sets off to explore the area north of the city. He hopes to find another "inland sea" that the men have heard about.

August 3, 1858	Speke discovers Lake Victoria. He believes it is the source of the Nile, but he cannot convince Burton.
March 4, 1859	Burton and Speke arrive back in Zanzibar to travel home.
May 9, 1859	Speke arrives in Britain and heads for London. He announces that he has discovered the source of the Nile. Everyone believes his claim and he becomes a national hero.
May 21, 1859	Burton arrives in Britain. He argues that Speke is wrong, but nobody listens.
April 27, 1860	Speke leaves Britain again to search for the Nile's starting point at Lake Victoria. A Scottish explorer, James Augustus Grant, goes with him.
August 15, 1860	Speke and Grant arrive in Zanzibar and start preparing for the journey to Lake Victoria.
September 30, 1860	Speke and Grant leave Zanzibar. They take a similar route to the one Speke and Burton had followed three years before.
January 25, 1861	Speke and Grant arrive in Tabora. When they leave, Grant gets sick and Speke has to leave him behind. The two men meet up again on the shores of Lake Victoria four months later.
July 28, 1862	Speke finally discovers Ripon Falls, where the Nile pours out of Lake Victoria. Grant is not with him, but the two men rejoin and head down the Nile for home.
February 13, 1863	Speke and Grant arrive at Gondokoro, Sudan. They meet Samuel and Florence Baker, from England, who are also exploring the Nile.
March 4, 1864	Samuel and Florence Baker discover Lake Albert.

Glossary

altitude height above sea level

botany scientific study of plants

colony settlement of people from one country living in another part of the world

compass instrument that helps people find their way. A compass contains a magnetic needle, which always points north.

conquer defeat and take over control of a group of people or a nation

empire group of countries controlled by another country. The British Empire was made up of many countries controlled by Great Britain.

Equator imaginary line that runs around the middle of Earth

expedition organized journey made by a group of people, usually to explore

famine great shortage of food, normally caused by a failure of crops. It can lead to hunger and starvation.

fever unusually high body temperature caused by disease. People with a fever often feel cold and shiver, even though they are very hot.

habitat natural surroundings in which a wild animal or plant lives. Types of habitat include forest, savannah, and desert.

hongo sort of tax paid to African chieftains or rulers by other people who wanted to cross their land

independent (countries) free from rule by foreign countries or governments

machete long-bladed hand tool used for chopping a path through thick vegetation

Mormon person who belongs to the Mormon religion, a branch of Christianity founded in 1830

mosque holy building where Muslims pray

mouth (of river) where a river flows into the sea

mutiny rebellion of soldiers against their commanders

opium type of drug made from the flower heads of poppies

plain large area of flat, grassy land with few trees

plateau area of flat land high above sea level

porter person who is paid to carry baggage

pride (of lions) name given to a group of lions that all live together

Royal Geographical Society British organization founded to increase the study of geography and improve our knowledge of the world through exploration

saber long sword with a curved blade

savannah open grassland in tropical parts of the world

settlement place where people live together, such as a village or town

source (of river) place where a river begins

steamer ship driven by a steam engine, usually powered by coal

sultan king of a Muslim country

Swahili language spoken in much of eastern and central Africa

trading post settlement built in a wild area for business or trade

translator person who understands two or more languages and can explain what a person speaking in a foreign language is saying

tropical to do with the tropics—the area between the Tropics of Cancer and Capricorn on a map of the world

vaccine medicine, usually given as a pill or injection, that prevents a person from later catching a particular disease

World Health Organization international organization that works to protect the health of the world's people

World War I war between Germany, Britain, Russia, and many other European countries, which lasted from 1914–1918. The United States joined the war in 1917.

Further Information

Books

Bowden, Rob. *Settlements of the River Nile.*
    Chicago: Heinemann Library, 2005.
Looks into the history of the towns and cities along the Nile River. Also explains how the river has been changed by human activity.

Noon, Steve, and Anne Millard. *The Story of the Nile.* New York: Dorling Kindersley, 2003.
A useful source for pictures and illustrations.

Shuter, Jane. *Life Along the Nile River.*
    Chicago: Heinemann Library, 2005.
Explains how the Nile River was important in history, including the part it played in the rise of the ancient Egyptian civilization.

Speke, John Hanning. *What Led to the Discovery of the Source of the Nile.* New York: BiblioBazaar, 2006.
The complete story of John Hanning Speke's journeys to discover the source of the Nile, written by the man himself.

Websites

Burton and Speke
www.bbc.co.uk/history/historic_figures/burton_sir_richard_francis.shtml
Tells the story of the life of Richard Francis Burton, both before and after his journeys to Africa.

www.bbc.co.uk/history/historic_figures/speke_john_hanning.shtml
Discusses John Hanning Speke's life, from his birth to his death.

Speke and Grant
www.touregypt.net/sourcec1.htm
All the details of Speke and Grant's journey to the source of the Nile, written by John Hanning Speke himself.

Places to Visit

The Field Museum
1400 S. Lake Shore Drive
Chicago, Illinois 60605-2496
Phone: (312) 922-9410
Website: www.fieldmuseum.org

The Field Museum features an exhibition hall about the Nile basin and the other areas of East Africa that Burton, Speke, and Grant explored. It also holds a recreation of a marsh on the Nile River.

The Metropolitan Museum of Art
1000 Fifth Avenue
New York, New York 10028
Phone: (212) 535-7710
Website: www.metmuseum.org

The Metropolitan Museum of Art has one of the world's most extensive collections of artifacts and art from the Nile basin and East Africa.

Index